EP Language Arts 1
Printables

This book belongs to:

_____

This book was made for your convenience. It is available for printing from the Easy Peasy All-in-One Homeschool website. It contains all of the printables from Easy Peasy's Language Arts 1 course. The instructions for each page are found in the online course.

Please note, in the various places where nouns are practiced, certain words like run, walk, fly, etc. are considered to be verbs. While there are instances where they can be nouns (you can go for a run, a fly can be a bug, etc.) this book assumes a more basic approach for this introductory level. If your child marks one of them as a noun, have a conversation with them to find out why.

Easy Peasy All-in-One Homeschool is a free online homeschool curriculum providing high quality education for children around the globe. It provides complete courses for preschool through high school graduation. For EP's curriculum visit allinonehomeschool.com.

EP Language Arts 1 Printables

This workbook, made by Tina Rutherford with permission from Easy Peasy All-in-One Homeschool, is based on the language arts component of Easy Peasy's curriculum. For EP's online curriculum visit allinonehomeschool.com

ISBN-13: 978-1535597494
ISBN-10: 1535597496

First Edition: August 2016

Long a

Use the words in the word box to fill in the blanks below. Each word is only used once. (NOTE: these worksheets must be used with the ONLINE course. They are NOT complete on their own.)

made	train	base	pail	brain	pain
	fail	fade	rain	shade	

Write four words that rhyme:

_____   _____

_____   _____

Write three words that rhyme:

_____   _____

_____

Write two words that rhyme:

_____   _____

Circle the remaining word in the word box.

Long a

Read each sentence and use a word from the word box to fill in the blank.

mail	rake	same	rain	bake

We used the _____ to get all of the leaves into a pile.

_____
- -
_____

I love to use my umbrella in the _____.

_____
- -
_____

I enjoy helping my mom _____ cupcakes.

_____
- -
_____

When I help with the laundry, I find two socks that are the _____.

_____
- -
_____

My grandma sent me a letter in the _____.

_____
- -
_____

Copywork

Copy this sentence onto the line below: *His wife shuddered.*

_____
- -
_____

Long e

Circle the long e words in the box below. Then find and circle them in the picture.

sun	sea	cloud	pole	reel	boat
reeds	bird	beak	hat	seat	
one	wheel	key	two	man	three

Long e

First, circle the words below that have the long e sound. Then write them in the blanks under the matching pictures.

tree	snake	bee	horse	leaf	bike
feet	egg	seal	pole	beach	

Copywork

Copy this sentence onto the line below: *So Jolly Robin thanked him.*

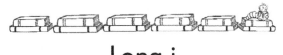

Long i

Read the story and fill in the blanks using the words below. Number the pictures in the order of the story.

bike	hide	find	slide	five	pile

I asked my brother to play a game of _____ and seek with me. I counted to _____, and then I went to _____ him. I looked behind the _____ in the garage. I rustled through the _____ of leaves. I finally found him under the _____.

☐   ☐   ☐   ☐

5

(This page left intentionally blank)

Long i

Sort the cupcakes! The girl wants the cupcakes with words that have a long i sound. The boy wants the rest of the cupcakes. Cut and paste the cupcakes in the right places.

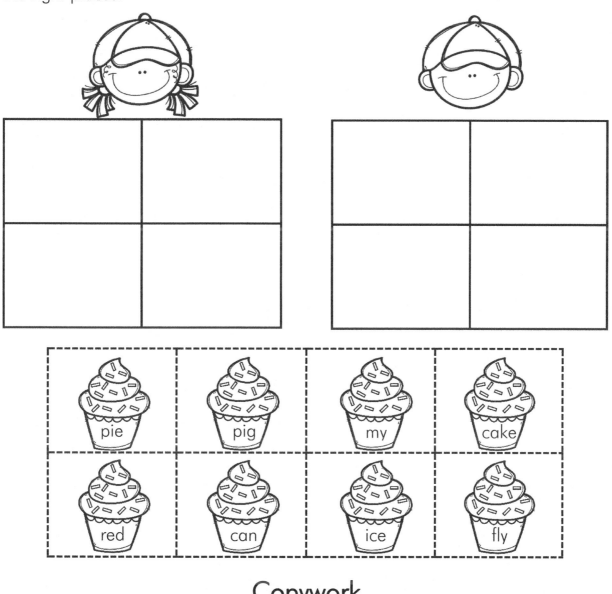

Copywork

Copy this sentence onto the lines below: *The struggle was over in a moment.*

(This page left intentionally blank)

Long o

Find and color all of the shapes with words that have the long o sound.

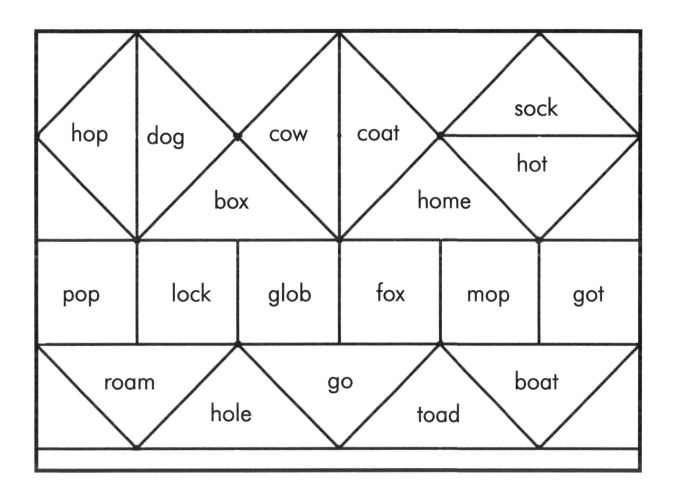

Copywork

Copy this sentence onto the lines below: *On some days there was no sun at all.*

Language Arts
Level 1

Long o

Read each sentence and use a word from the word box to fill in the blank.

| bone | hose | snow | boat |

I love to play in the _____.

My dog's favorite treat is a _____.

I watered my flowers with the _____.

I play with my toy _____ in the bathtub.

Copywork

Copy this sentence onto the lines below: *His wife, however, shook her head.*

Long u

Read the story and fill in the blanks using the words below.

clue	two	do	blue	you	glue

I made a card for my sister who turned _____. I didn't have a _____ what to make. Then my mom got out the _____ so I could make a glitter picture. I chose _____, her favorite color. I wrote the words, "Happy birthday to _____." It's fun to see all she is learning to _____.

Copywork

Copy this sentence onto the lines below: *He had expected to have a ride.*

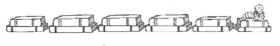

Long u

Let's make some stew! Color in the vegetables that have words with the long u sound in them.

Write two lines of rhyming poem using two of the long u words above.

_____
- -
_____
- -
_____

Copywork

Copy this sentence onto the lines below: *And Jolly Robin did not laugh.*

(This page left intentionally blank)

The Boy Who Cried Wolf

Cut out the following blocks and arrange them in the order they happened in the story.

The boy saw a wolf.	The father told his son to have no more drills.
The boy thought he saw the shadow of a wolf.	No one came to help.
The boy decided the villagers needed to practice a wolf drill.	The boy's father asked him to watch the sheep.

(This page left intentionally blank)

Copywork

Copy this sentence onto the lines below: *I'd like to hear you sing.*

Copywork

Copy this sentence onto the lines below: *And so all the weeping he might do would be merely wasted.*

Language Arts
Level 1

Lesson
15

Goldilocks and the Three Bears

Cut out the following blocks and arrange them in the order they happened in the story.

The chair broke into pieces.

The three bears came home.

Goldilocks screamed and ran out of the house.

Goldilocks followed the bird into the forest.

Goldilocks tasted cobbler that was too hot.

Goldilocks fell asleep.

Copywork

Copy this sentence onto the lines below: *His cousin shook his head at that.*

(This page left intentionally blank)

Mystery S Picture

Color the words that end in an "s" sound blue. Color the words that end in a "z" sound green.

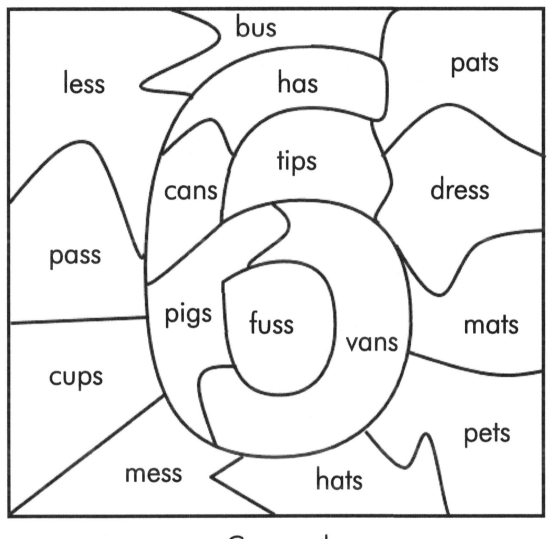

Copywork

Copy this sentence onto the lines below: *The feathered folk in Pleasant Valley were all aflutter.*

_____

- -

_____

- -

_____

- -

_____

Ending Blends

Read the story and fill in the blanks using the blends in the box below.

| nt | pt | nk | nd | sk | st |

I wanted to do my mom a favor while she **sle**____. First, I cleaned all of the dishes in the **si**____. Next, I **we**____ to **a**____ my sister if she needed help with her math. It is my **be**____ subject. Finally, I put away all of the toys I could **fi**____. My mom was pleased!

Copywork

Copy this sentence onto the lines below: *But all the others gazed at him in amazement.*

Beginning Blends

Fill in the blanks beside each picture with its beginning blend from the box. Try to fully write at least two of the words.

| ch | dr | fl | pr | sk | sl | sn | tr | str | thr |

Copy this sentence onto the lines below: *Several times Jasper tried.*

Ch sound

Circle the word in each row that *begins* with the same sound as . Then write them neatly on the line.

chain

beach

basket

sheep

child

bird

_____

Circle the word in each row that *ends* with the same sound as ⌚. Then write them neatly on the line.

bench

fox

fish

cupcake

peach

pencil

_____

Copy this sentence onto the lines below: *Mr. Crow looked up quickly.*

_____

Ck sound

Circle the words that contain the "ck" sound in the box below. Then find and circle them in the picture. Finally, write them on the line.

| duck | arch | lock | beach | clock | neck | art |

Copywork

Copy this sentence onto the lines below: *Mr. Crow was more than willing.*

Show me the Treasure!

Color brown the words that begin with the same beginning sound in 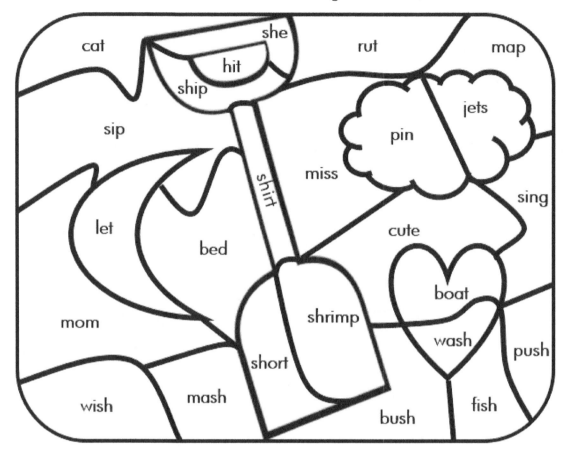. Color yellow the ones that end with the same ending sound in _____. Color the rest blue.

cat
she
hit
ship
rut
map
jets
sip
pin
shirt
miss
sing
let
bed
cute
boat
mom
shrimp
wash
push
short
wish
mash
fish
bush

Write two words that begin with "sh" and two words that end with "sh" on the line below.

_____
- -
_____

Copywork

Copy this sentence onto the lines below: *That was unfortunate for the mice.*

_____
- -
_____
- -
_____

Hard and soft th

The girl wants the cupcakes with words that have a hard th like the word *this*. The boy wants the cupcakes with the soft th like the word *thank*. Cut and paste the cupcakes in the right places. Then write 5 "th" words on the lines.

Copy this sentence onto the lines below: *It was a really good thing for Solomon Owl.*

(This page left intentionally blank)

Who Whistled?

Circle the words in the word box that begin with the same sound as . Then find those words in the puzzle below. Finally, write them on the lines.

wheel	ship	chop	whale	shape	wheat
plum	whisk	draw	whistle	school	treat

W H I S K A N T L
A H N Q D Z A E S
M R P W H A L E P
U W T A I O W W A
L H O Z L T H Z T
P E P T R T I I S
W E R Y U A S H A
H L O H F E T N D
E D X E W A L M S
A Q R U L I E V U
T Y P T O M A L B

Trigraphs

Choose the correct trigraph from the box below to make each word complete and finish the story. Then write three of the completed words on the lines.

thr   shr

My sister and I played a game of catch. I ___**ew** the ball to her. Instead of catching it, she ___**ieked** and jumped out of the way. The ball landed in the ___**ub**. I asked her if she was going to catch the ball. She ___**ugged** and said, "I get ___**ee** strikes, right?" On my next ___**ow** she caught the ball and said, "What a ___**ill**!"

_____

_____

_____

Silent e

Help the gingerbread boy get to the gingerbread house. If you come to a word with a silent e and a long vowel sound, go left ⬅. If you come to a word with a short vowel sound, go right ➡. Then write four silent e words on the lines.

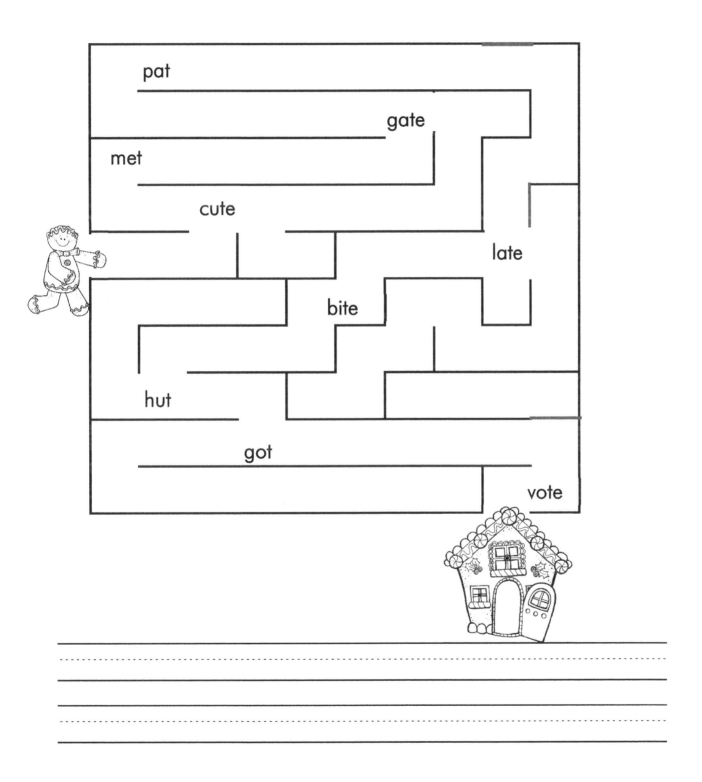

Main Idea

Circle the sentence that best describes the main idea for each picture.

The penguin is a dancer.

The penguin is an artist.

The caterpillar is friendly.

The caterpillar is mean.

The girl is afraid.

The girl is happy.

Ending Punctuation

Circle the punctuation that should go at the end of each sentence.

My mom is going to the store to buy milk

.   ?   !

Watch out for that snake

.   ?   !

What time is it

.   ?   !

I can't wait for my birthday

.   ?   !

My favorite animal at the zoo was the leopard

.   ?   !

What color is your bike

.   ?   !

Copywork

Copy this sentence onto the lines below: *Then Solomon sat up and listened.*

_____

- -

_____

- -

_____

Capital I

Rewrite the sentences so that they are correct. Remember that the letter I is always capitalized when it is by itself as the word I.

Do you know how old i am?

_____

i love to go to the park.

_____

My friends and i like to play games.

_____

i love my family.

_____

i am special.

_____

Is or Are

Fill in the blanks with either **is** or **are**. Read the sentence out loud to figure out which word fits best.

Today _____ my sister's birthday.

We _____ going to the park.

The park _____ her favorite place.

We _____ having ice cream.

Her favorite flavor _____ mint.

My favorite _____ chocolate chip.

We _____ going to have fun!

Is or Are

Fill in the blanks with either **is** or **are**. Use *is* if the sentence is about one thing.
Use *are* if the sentence is about more than one thing.

The traffic _____ heavy today.

The cars _____ moving slowly.

A bus _____ at the front.

It _____ stopping.

People _____ getting on the bus.

The vehicles _____ moving again.

Copywork

Copy this sentence onto the lines below: *"What have you been eating?" she inquired.*

_____

_____

Long and Short a

Color in the spaces with words with a short a sound blue. Color in the spaces with words with a long a sound gray. What long a sound picture do you see?

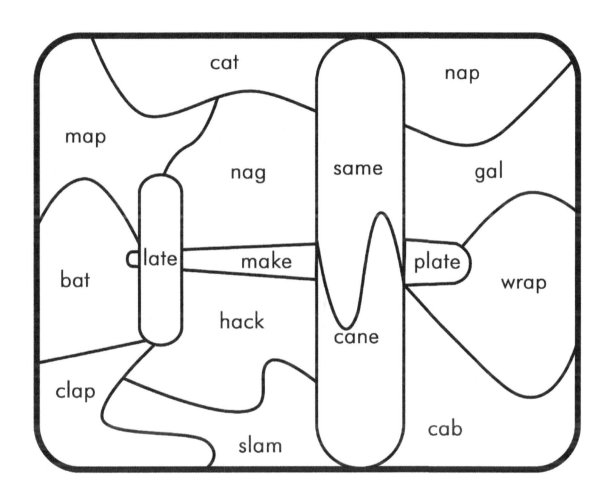

cat

nap

map

nag

same

gal

late

make

plate

bat

hack

cane

wrap

clap

slam

cab

Copywork

Copy this sentence onto the lines below: *"Good!" she exclaimed with a smile.*

_____

- -

_____

- -

_____

Long and Short e

Put all the words with the short e sound in the box with the bed. Put all of the words with the long e sound in the box with the feet.

get	meal	seat	mess	sell
team	ten	bead	seek	gel

Copywork

Copy this sentence onto the lines below: *It was different with Benjamin Bat.*

Long and Short i

For each sentence, choose the word that best fits and write it on the line.

My dog _____ his toy.   bit   bite

The gum cost a _____.   dim   dime

I love to _____.   slid   slide

We have a _____ tree.   pin   pine

A bird is on the _____.   limb   lime

We already _____ a match.   lit   lite

I _____ the color blue.   lick   like

(This page left intentionally blank)

Long and Short o

Sort the cupcakes! The girl wants the cupcakes with words that have a short o sound. The boy wants the cupcakes with the long o sound. Cut and paste the cupcakes.

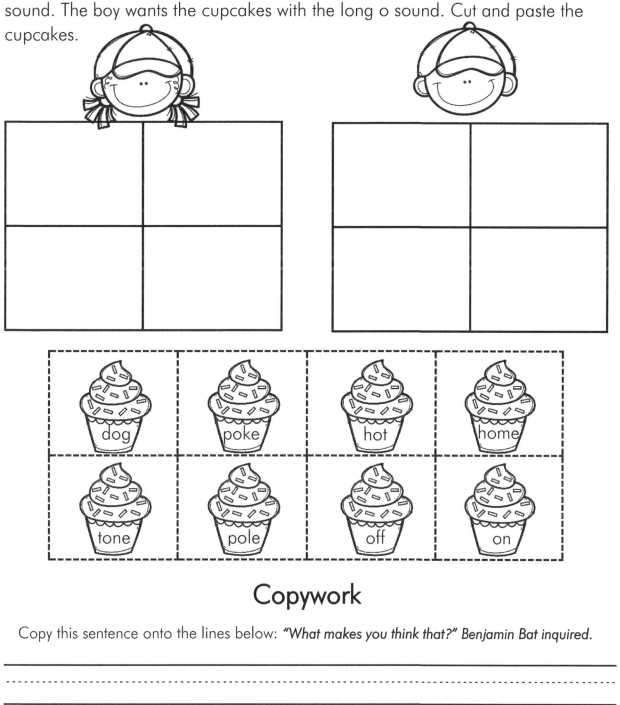

Copywork

Copy this sentence onto the lines below: *"What makes you think that?" Benjamin Bat inquired.*

(This page left intentionally blank)

Long and Short u

Put all the words with the short u sound in the box with the hut. Put all of the words with the long u sound in the box with the cube.

mutt	pup	chute	rug	tube
cute	prune	hug	duke	cup

Copywork

Copy this sentence onto the lines below: *"Oh, I shall be willing to step outside," Solomon told him.*

Punctuation

Fill in the punctuation mark that best fits each sentence.

I'm so scared

What is your name

My dog likes to run and play

How are you today

Stop

Watch out

My favorite subject is math

What is your favorite subject

Copywork

Copy this sentence onto the lines below: *"You surely ought to be glad to please your own cousin,"*
he told Simon.

_____
- -
_____
- -
_____
- -
_____

Ar Blend

These "ar" words are scrambled! Unscramble them and then find them in the puzzle below. Use the pictures for hints if you need them.

| arkb | rac | rkahs | rcta | trad | thacr |

```
C  H  A  R  T  A  N  T  L
A  Z  N  Q  D  Z  A  E  S
R  C  G  A  N  M  N  L  H
U  A  H  C  B  A  R  K  A
B  R  N  D  A  R  T  Z  R
P  T  A  T  K  N  O  I  K
C  E  P  Y  U  A  F  H  A
```

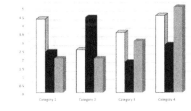

Can you think of any other "ar" words? Write them below.

_____

- -

_____

- -

_____

Blends: ir, ur, er

Fill in the blank with the proper blend from the box.

ir	ur	er

I like __t__key__ and gravy.

I got __th__d__ place in the race.

Do you like beef __j__ky__?

Dancers like to spin and __tw__l__.

The farmer __ch__ned__ the butter.

Or sound

Circle the words that contain the "or" sound in the box below. Then find and circle them in the picture.

| fork | barn | curl | shorts | horn | storm | art |

Make inferences! Circle the answer that best fits. Explain to someone why you chose the answer you did.

Andrew put on his pajamas.

1) It was bedtime.   2) He was cold.   3) It was morning.

Jessica dropped the mail and it swirled around the driveway.

1) It was hot.   2) It was windy.   3) It was raining.

Her hair was soft and clean.

1) She was running.   2) She was sleeping.   3) She just had a bath.

(This page left intentionally blank)

Where's My Tire?

The trucks are missing their tires! Cut and paste the tires with words that rhyme with "tire" onto the trucks. Then write "fire" and 3 words that rhyme with it.

fire   hare

pure   hire

wire   bear

share   liar

sire   higher

(This page left intentionally blank)

Reader Bear

Mr. Bear only wants to read books with words that rhyme with his name. Color in the books that rhyme with "bear." Then write five words that rhyme with bear. Can you think of any new ones?

square   there   hair

soar   doctor   share

pear   floor   chair

_____

_____

_____

A-B-C

Get the bookworm to the rest of the books! Start with the capital A in the top row and then move to the B and on through the alphabet in order. Once you get to Z, move to the lowercase a and keep continuing through the alphabet until you find the books.

X	R	L	A	B	C	L	K
Q	T	S	O	E	D	Z	Y
J	I	H	G	F	J	K	S
K	B	G	J	L	C	N	P
L	M	Q	S	U	W	Y	A
I	N	O	P	Q	T	K	Z
O	R	E	S	R	D	B	V
F	X	H	T	C	F	H	M
C	E	D	U	V	W	X	J
A	R	G	S	L	Z	Y	T
n	q	h	s	m	a	b	c
b	w	a	y	r	g	f	d
e	d	o	q	u	k	t	e
p	r	j	c	n	x	g	f
v	y	l	k	j	i	h	c
i	u	m	n	o	p	b	l
b	d	i	s	f	q	r	s
p	v	o	x	w	v	u	t
z	x	t	y	l	g	z	a
a	h	e	z	j	m	w	k

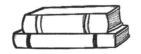

A-B-C

Circle the first letter of each word. Cut the strips out and lay the words out in alphabetical order.

fork

- - - - - - - - - - - - - - - - - - - -

carrot

- - - - - - - - - - - - - - - - - - - -

 egg

- - - - - - - - - - - - - - - - - - - -

apple

- - - - - - - - - - - - - - - - - - - -

drink

- - - - - - - - - - - - - - - - - - - -

banana

(This page left intentionally blank)

Speech Practice

Read through these knock knock jokes and choose several to read aloud to someone. Use your voice to show which sentences end in a period, which end in a question mark, and which end in an exclamation point. If you're not sure how to do that, ask a parent before you begin.

Knock, knock.
Who's there?
Ash.
Ash who?
Bless you!

Knock, knock.
Who's there?
Orange.
Orange who?
Orange you thankful for Easy Peasy
All-in-One Homeschool?

Knock, knock.
Who's there?
Shower.
Shower who?
Shower is hot today!

Knock, knock.
Who's there?
Dogs go.
Dogs go who?
No, dogs go "woof"!

Knock, knock.
Who's there?
Olive.
Olive who?
Olive you!

Knock, knock.
Who's there?
Annie.
Annie who?
Annie body home?

Knock, knock.
Who's there?
Needle.
Needle who?
Needle little time to come up with
more jokes.

Knock, knock.
Who's there?
Canoe.
Canoe who?
Canoe come here for a minute?

Knock, knock.
Who's there?
Harry.
Harry who?
Harry up, it's cold out here!

Knock, knock.
Who's there?
Megan.
Megan who?
Megan end to these knock knock
jokes!

Weather Words

Fill in the blanks using the words in the word box. Pay attention to the clues you get in the sentences to decide which word goes in the blank. Then describe your favorite season.

| drizzle | freezing | humid | crisp |

It is so hot and _____ this summer! I know some people love it, but I'm looking forward to fall and the cool, _____ air. In winter when the air is downright _____, I love to snuggle up under a blanket by the fire. Of course, during the spring it's so peaceful to open my window and listen to the falling _____. I guess each season has its perks!

_____
_____
_____
_____

My Favorite Room

Use this brainstorming page to describe your favorite room. Start by filling in the main idea blank, then fill in the boxes below.

Main idea:

My favorite room is _____

Looks like	Sounds like	Smells like

Tastes like	Feels like	Makes me feel

What Happened?

Write a silly story about this picture. How did this happen?

What Happened?

Write a silly story about these pictures. Why was the ladybug sad? What happened to make it happy again?

Copywork

Copy this sentence: *Jolly Robin's worrying wife wouldn't give him a moment's peace.*

That sentence said "worrying wife." Both words started with a W. Can you think of another pair of words that start with the same letter? For example: **Jolly Robin's sad son.**

Now write a new sentence using the words you chose. For example: **Jolly Robin's sad son said he wanted to play.**

Copywork

Copy this sentence: *Jolly Robin told his wife how he swooped down over Reddy Woodpecker's head.*

Picture Jolly Robin flying over Reddy Woodpecker. Now picture him swooping down over him. Which is more exciting? Can you write an exciting sentence?

Copywork

Copy this sentence: *One day Reddy Woodpecker was tap, tap, tapping on a tall poplar that grew beside the brook.*

_____
- -
_____
- -
_____
- -
_____
- -

"Tap" is a word that sounds like its name. Can you think of other words that sound like their name? Buzz, pop, swish. What are some others? Can you write a sentence using a sound word?

_____
- -
_____
- -
_____
- -
_____
- -

Describing the Setting

Think about your book again. Write description words about where the main character lives or where the story takes place. Fill in the boxes below with words that tell what you would see, feel, hear, smell, and taste if you were where the story takes place.

Looks like	Sounds like	Smells like

Tastes like	Feels like	Makes me feel

Copywork

Copy this sentence onto the lines below: *Reddy Woodpecker had no patience with him.*

_____
- -
_____

_____
- -
_____

Copywork

Copy this sentence onto the lines below: *It's no wonder Reddy was angry.*

_____

- -

_____

_____

- -

_____

Copywork

Copy this sentence onto the lines below: *Then Frisky sat on a limb and glared at him.*

Copywork

Copy this sentence onto the lines below: *Frisky did not intend to go hungry when winter came.*

_____

- -

_____

_____

- -

_____

Punctuation

Fill in the punctuation mark that best fits each sentence.

I'm so excited

When is your birthday

My sister loves to sing

I enjoy dancing

Help

What is your favorite food

How old are you

Spelling

Fill in the missing letter.

g__rl

i u e o

f__om

l r y a

pr__y

o i a u

h__nt

a o u e

cav__

u l e r

do__n

e z a w

I or Me

Fill in the blank with **I** or **me** to make the sentence correct.

_____ just baked my first cake.

Come with _____ to the kitchen.

_____ will show you my cake.

You can tell _____ what you think.

_____ think it looks delicious.

Will you eat it with _____?

Spelling

Play a game of hangman. Cross off the letters as you guess them to keep track.

a b c d e f g h i j k l m n o p q r s t u v w x y z

__ __ __ __ __

Capital I

Rewrite the sentences so that they are correct. Then practice your spelling by finding the words from the box in the puzzle at the bottom of the page.

i love spaghetti.

_____

- -

_____

Do you think i am smart?

_____

- -

_____

i always try my best.

_____

- -

_____

May i go first?

_____

- -

_____

```
F A P A R T P T L
I C N Q D Z I R P
L R G I F T N Y U
L W H I P A E P R
B I N D E N X Z X
P C A L L T A R S
```

| fill | gift | whip | pine | try | call | trap |

Capitalization

Underline the words in each sentence that need to be capitalized. Remember that all names are capitalized – names of people, places, days, months, etc. Also remember that each sentence should start with a capital letter. Then use the lines at the bottom to write your spelling words.

the children were excited for their trip to the zoo on friday.

mr. smith brought the ham for our easter meal.

the fire station is on main street.

mary's favorite holiday is christmas.

in july we see a lot of fireworks.

Copywork

Copy this sentence onto the line below (pay attention to the punctuation): *No, it wasn't that.*

_____

- -

_____

Copywork

Copy this sentence onto the lines below: *Old Mr. Toad just laughed.*

_____

- -

_____

_____

- -

_____

Copywork

Copy this sentence onto the lines below: *By and by he turned his head.*

_____

- -

_____

_____

- -

_____

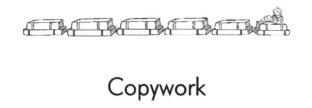

Copywork

Copy this sentence onto the line below: *"Next time I'll get him!"*

_____

- -

_____

Copywork

Copy these words onto the lines below: *ship shop shape shine shirt shoe*

_____

- -

_____

_____

- -

_____

Different Nouns

A **noun** is a person, place or thing. There are different types of nouns. Copy the word into the blanks as you learn about nouns.

Common nouns:

girl

church

Proper nouns: name a *specific* person, place or thing

Carol

Calvary

Collective nouns: name a *group* of people, places or things

family

congregation

Fill in the missing "sh" to complete the spelling words below.

___ape   ___ine   ___ip

___irt   ___op

Copy this sentence onto the line below: *"That's good," said she.*

Sh words

Complete the crossword puzzle using the clues below.

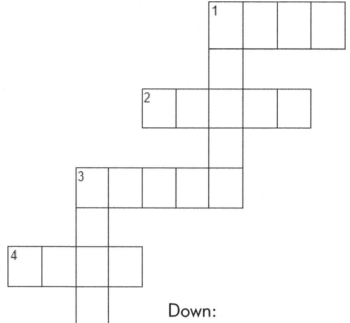

Across:
1. a big boat
2. can have long or short sleeves
3. a square is an example
4. you wear it over your sock

Down:
1. the sun can do this
3. what you do when you need to buy something

Underline the nouns in the sentences below:

There is wind blowing the trees.

A big bus drove through the streets.

A spider crawled across the deck.

The baseball crashed through the window.

Copywork

Copy these words onto the lines below: *chin chip chop cheap church churn*

_____

- -

_____

_____

- -

_____

Noun Hunt

Underline all of the nouns in this sentence.

His big eyes filled with tears as he looked at Danny

Meadow Mouse for Danny was all torn and hurt by

the cruel claws of Hooty the Owl, and you know Peter

has a very tender heart.

Fill in the missing ch from the words below.

____in   ____ip

____op   ____eap

____urch   ____urn

Copywork

Copy this sentence onto the lines below: *So Peter hurried over to the nearest tree.*

_____

- -

_____

_____

- -

_____

Find the Nouns

Underline the nouns in the following sentences.

Mary took the letter to the post office.

Jennifer went to the movie theater with her friends.

Michael sat on the swing next to his cousin.

David ate the apple at the table.

Charlie put tomatoes on his salad.

Jamie took her sister to the zoo.

Jason got mustard on his shirt.

Copywork

Copy these words onto the lines below: *who what why where when which*

_____

_____

_____

Proper Nouns

Proper nouns are names of people, places, or things. Underline the proper nouns in the following sentences.

Mr. Davis went to Pittsburgh last Sunday.

My brother, Stephen, works at McDonald's.

Rachel took a jog in Central Park.

Clara went to school at Lincoln Elementary.

Natalie's birthday is Saturday.

Fill in the missing wh from the words below.

___o   ___en

___at   ___ere

___y   ___ich

Copywork

Copy this sentence onto the lines below: *Peter Rabbit sat in his secretest place in the dear Old Briar-patch.*

_____
- -
_____
_____
- -
_____

Find the Proper Nouns

Underline the proper nouns in the following sentences.

The Empire State Building is really tall.

Jenn got a purple hat on Wednesday.

Tim used his telescope to see Jupiter.

April is such a rainy month.

The Grand Canyon is in Arizona.

Amy lives on the corner of Lake Avenue and Elm Street.

Avery lives in California.

Copywork

Copy these words onto the lines below: *this that they thing think there*

Th Words

Fill in the missing th from the words below.

__is

__ing

__at

__ink

__ey

__ere

Can you think of six proper nouns? Remember to capitalize them!

_____
- -
_____

_____
- -
_____

_____
- -
_____

_____
- -
_____

_____
- -
_____

_____
- -
_____

Copywork

Copy these words onto the lines below: *this thing where why shop shoe chop church*

- -

- -

Copywork

Copy these plural words onto the lines below: *bikes stores cars tables friends times*

_____

- -

_____

_____

- -

_____

Copywork

Copy these plural words onto the lines below: *washes misses brushes peaches*
wishes taxes

_____

- -

_____

_____

- -

_____

Language Arts
Level 1

Lesson
138

Copywork

Copy these plural words onto the lines below: *toys ways days plays keys*

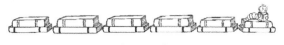

Plurals

Make the following words plural.

bike_____   wash_____

store_____   baby_____

friend_____   day_____

miss_____   time_____

peach_____   tax_____

try_____   way_____

play_____   table_____

brush_____   wish_____

Circle the pronouns below.

it   flower   she   they

pencil   her   him   shirt

Copywork

Copy this sentence onto the lines below: *Who makes an enemy a friend, to fear and worry puts an end.*

Copywork

Copy this sentence onto the lines below: *There the same thing happened.*

Copywork

Copy this sentence onto the lines below: *A sudden odd surprise made Farmer Brown's boy's hair to rise.*

Copywork

Copy this sentence onto the line below: *"What is it?"*

Copywork

Copy this sentence onto the line below: *"That's a splendid idea!"*

- -

Plurals

Make the following words plural. As a reminder, if Y comes after a vowel, just add S. If Y comes after a consonant (any letter that's not a vowel), change the Y to I and add ES.

Write the vowels on this line for easy reference:

_____

cherry _____   army _____

party _____   play _____

tray _____   boy _____

berry _____   fairy _____

penny _____   day _____

fly _____   copy _____

Copywork

Write a silly sentence using one or more of the words above.

_____
_____
_____

Plural Rules

The regular plural of nouns is made by adding an S to the end of the word. As we've learned, there are exceptions to this rule. We call these exceptions **irregular plurals**. Let's review what we've learned.

We make the plural of nouns that end in CH, SH, X, or SS by adding ES.

one dress
two dresses

one fox
two foxes

one couch
two couches

We make the plural of some nouns that end in F or FE by changing the F or FE to V and adding ES.

one leaf
two leaves

one elf
two elves

We make the plural of nouns that end in Y not following a vowel by changing the Y to I and adding ES.

one cherry
two cherries

one fly
two flies

We make the plural of some OO nouns by changing the OO to EE.

one foot
two feet

one goose
two geese

And of course, there are many words that just don't follow a rule.

Find the plurals:

knife _____

box _____

try _____

boy _____

miss _____

man _____

Write a sentence about your favorite place. Start it like this: *My favorite place to be is...*

_____

_____

_____

Copywork

Copy this part of the poem onto the lines below: *All things bright and beautiful*

_____

_____

_____

_____

Copywork

Copy this part of the poem onto the lines below: *All creatures great and small*

_____

- -

_____

_____

- -

_____

Copywork

Copy this part of the poem onto the lines below: *All things wise and wonderful*

_____

- -

_____

_____

- -

_____

Copywork

Copy this part of the poem onto the lines below: *The Lord God made them all.*

Copywork

Copy this part of the poem onto the lines below: *He gave us eyes to see them,*

Copywork

Copy this part of the poem onto the lines below: *And lips that we might tell*

_____

- -

_____

_____

- -

_____

Copywork

Copy this part of the poem onto the lines below: *How great is God Almighty,*

Copywork

Copy this part of the poem onto the lines below: *Who has made all things well.*

Comic Book

Create your own comic book! If you need more sections, draw lines vertically (up and down) to further section off the rectangles. You will have more pages and more days to work on this.

Comic Book

Continue to work on your comic book.

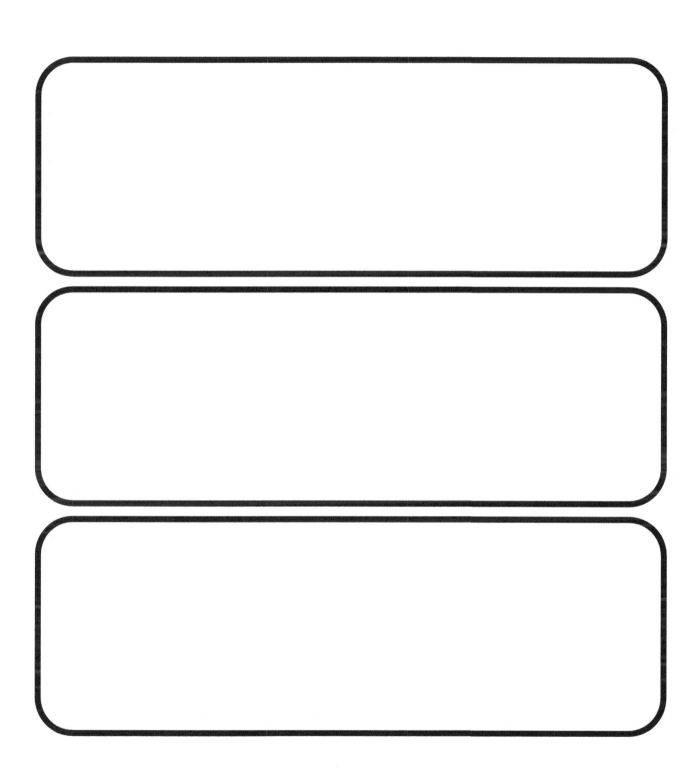

Comic Book

Continue to work on your comic book.

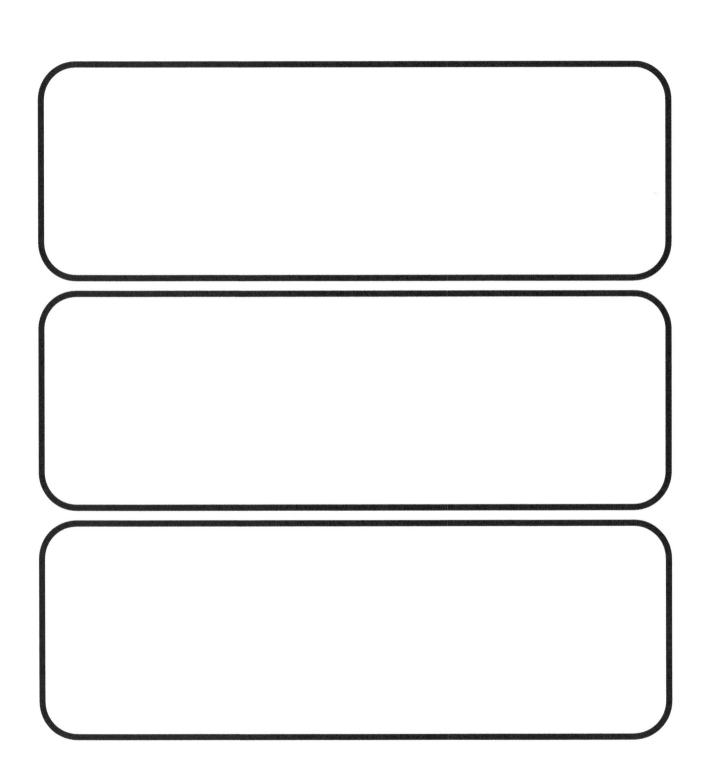

Comic Book

Continue to work on your comic book.

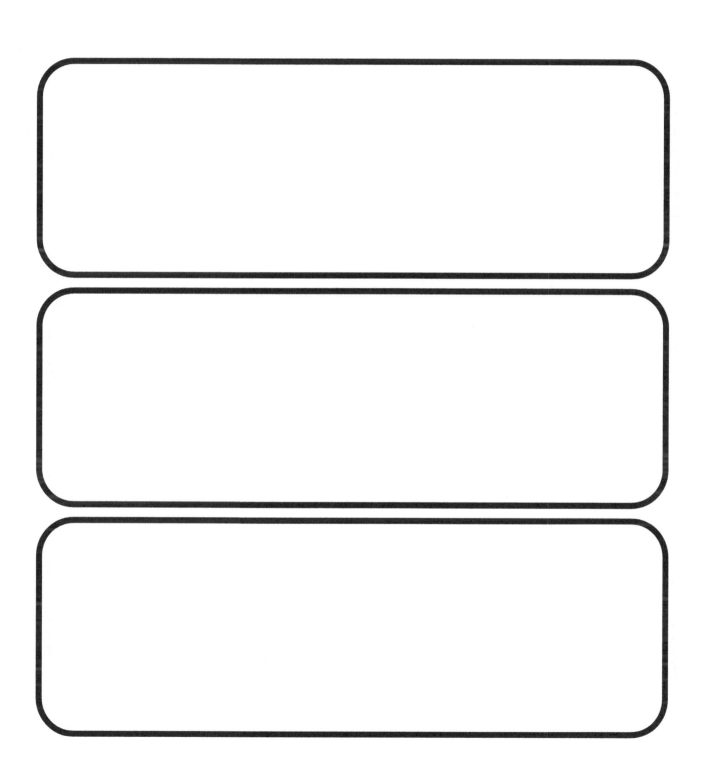

Comic Book

Finish your comic book. Read it aloud to a parent or sibling.

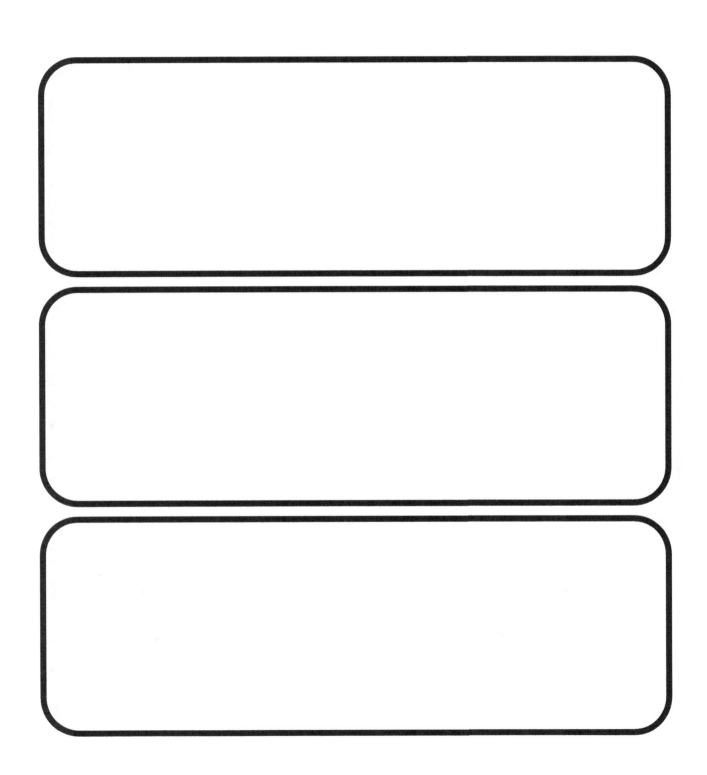

The Easy Peasy All-in-One Homeschool is a free, complete online homeschool curriculum. There are 180 days of ready-to-go assignments for every level and every subject. It's created for your children to work as independently as you want them to. Preschool through high school is available as well as courses ranging from English, math, science and history to art, music, computer, thinking, physical education and health. A daily Bible lesson is offered as well. The mission of Easy Peasy is to enable those to homeschool who otherwise thought they couldn't.

The Genesis Curriculum takes the Bible and turns it into lessons for your homeschool. Daily lessons include Bible reading, memory verse, spelling, handwriting, vocabulary, grammar, Biblical language, science, social studies, writing, and thinking through discussion questions.

The Genesis Curriculum uses a complete book of the Bible for one full year. The curriculum is being made using both Old and New Testament books. Find us online at genesiscurriculum.com to read about the latest developments in this expanding curriculum.

Made in the USA
Monee, IL
11 June 2023

35612685R00063